Lunch for Tig

Paul Shipton
Illustrated by Clive Scruton

Oxford

The children were eating lunch.

Tig was very hungry.
"Where is my lunchbox?" he said.

Everyone looked for Tig's lunchbox. They couldn't find it.

"Here," said Emma.
   She gave Tig a cheese sandwich.

"Yuck!" said Tig.
He didn't like cheese.

Sam gave Tig some crisps.

"YUCK!" said Tig.
He didn't like crisps.

Meg gave Tig a banana.

"**YUCK!**" said Tig.
He didn't like bananas either.

Tig ate the banana skin.
"Not bad," he said.

Tig bit the table.
"That's good," he said.

Tig's mum came to school.

"Here's your lunchbox," said Tig's mum.

Tig ate his lunch.